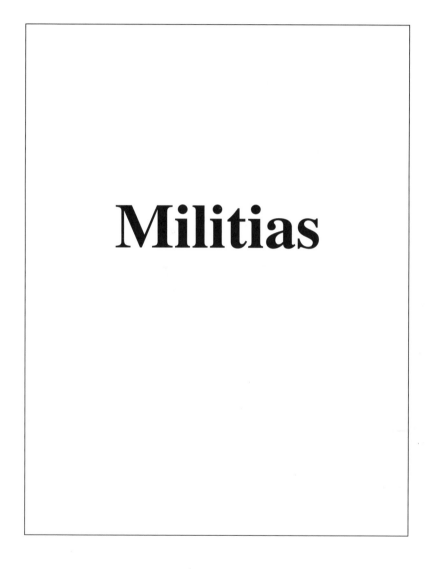

Militias

Look for these and other books in the Lucent Overview Series:

Militias

by Gail B. Stewart

LUCENT
BOOKS

LUCENT Overview Series

Library of Congress Cataloging-in-Publication Data

Stewart, Gail, 1949–
    Militias / by Gail B. Stewart.
        p.   cm. — (Lucent overview series)
    Includes bibliographical references and index.
    Summary: Discusses the rise of the anti-government militia
movement in the United States, the involvement of militias with
white supremacists and other hate groups, and the connections
between these groups and such events as the Oklahoma City bombing.
    ISBN 1-56006-501-X (alk. paper)
    1. Militia movements—United States—Juvenile literature.
    2. Right-wing extremists—United States—Juvenile literature.
    3. Government, Resistance to—United States—Juvenile literature.
    [1. Militia movements.   2. Right-wing extremists.   3. Political
    crimes and offenses.]   I. Title.   II. Series.
    HN90.R3S64   1998
    322.4'2'0973—dc21   97–23362
                                                                   CIP
                                                                    AC

Copyright © 1998 by Lucent Books, Inc.
P.O. Box 289011, San Diego, CA 92198-9011
Printed in the U.S.A.

Contents

Introduction

DOWNSTAIRS IN THE dining room of the little South Dakota church, scores of men are standing around in small groups. Most are dressed in blue jeans and flannel shirts; a few wear old army fatigues. Many wear brimmed caps, some displaying the name of a tractor or farm implement dealer. The men are talking and drinking coffee out of paper cups. The conversation ranges from business concerns to their children's progress in school. Occasionally someone tells a funny story and a burst of laughter erupts from the group.

At first, an observer might assume they are here for a farmers' organization meeting, or perhaps a rural political caucus. But as the men take their seats and the meeting is called to order, it is clear that this is an altogether different sort of gathering. They have come together as they do twice a month—some from as far as three hundred miles away—to train as soldiers of a private army. After a brief discussion of battle tactics and strategy, the men will arm themselves and practice maneuvers in the woods—maneuvers, they say, that they will probably need in the months ahead.

In all fifty states

This citizens' army, or militia, is one of many training and operating throughout the United States; conservative estimates by federal and state law enforcement agencies of militia membership range from the tens to the hundreds of thousands.

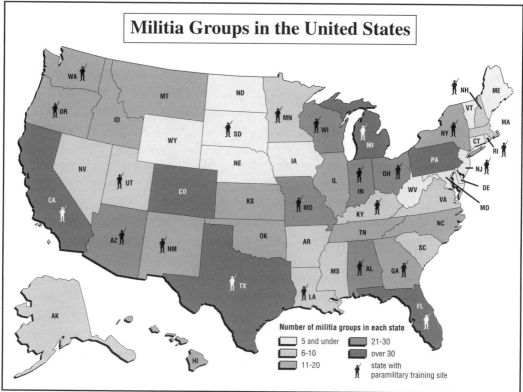

Militia Groups in the United States

Number of militia groups in each state
- 5 and under
- 6-10
- 11-20
- 21-30
- over 30
- state with paramilitary training site

Source: Klanwatch Project, 1996

"Nobody knows for sure," admits one federal marshal,

> because new militias are cropping up all the time. By their very nature, these militias are secret; they aren't broadcasting their membership. But our best estimates [as of late 1996] say that there are at least 400 militias that we know about—and that's not including some of the "secret cells"—these little commando squadrons—that we've only heard rumors of. We also know that there is militia activity in all 50 states.

Not all militias are as small or localized as the one in western South Dakota, according to a government agent.

> Some of them are really tiny, with fewer than 50 members, but we know of some that have membership in the thousands, like the Michigan Militia, or the Militia of Montana—we're estimating that one has at least 20,000 card-carrying members. And then you add to that the hundreds of thousands of other people who maybe don't belong, but who are sympathetic to the ideas of the militia, and all of a sudden that's a lot of people we're talking about.

These men are members of a militia group called the Wolverines. The FBI increased its interest in militias after the Oklahoma City bombing in 1995.

"A wake-up call for law enforcement"

A citizen militia practicing shooting and basic combat maneuvers in the last years of the twentieth century, when "war" in most Western societies means high-tech missiles and nuclear bombs, seems like a throwback to a less sophisticated era. What possible interest could government agencies have in keeping tabs on men who spend two weekends each month playing war games?

The answer, say the Federal Bureau of Investigation (FBI) and other law enforcement agencies, can be summed up in two words: Oklahoma City. After the April 19, 1995, bombing of the federal building there killed 169 people, Americans were horrified to learn that the act may have been committed not by foreign terrorists, but by fellow Americans. Convicted of the bombing in June 1997, Timothy James McVeigh, is an avowed racist and was affiliated both with neo-Nazi groups and with brigades of the Michigan Militia.

"Looking at the agenda these groups have—especially the militias, which have the firepower to act on their anger at their enemies—the militias were found to be much more than people originally thought," says one expert.

It's as though we turned over the rock, and instead of seeing a bunch of harmless eccentrics in camouflage suits, we find a lot of highly organized groups with strong ties to what we think of as hate groups—neo-Nazi, white supremacist, antigovernment, and so on. Many of these militias have large stockpiles of very sophisticated weapons. It was a wake-up call for law enforcement in this country.

"A recipe for disaster"

Signs of deep anger and even hate can be seen in the literature and the speeches of militia leaders. One popular militia circular is a poster of President Bill Clinton and Hillary Clinton, stamped "WANTED DEAD OR ALIVE—FOR TREASON AGAINST AMERICA" in big black letters. Another proclaims, "MAKE THE WORLD A LITTLE SAFER FOR YOUR KIDS—KILL A FED."

The remnants of the Alfred P. Murrah Federal Building in Oklahoma City after the 1995 bombing. Convicted bomber Timothy McVeigh was a member of a militant militia group while he plotted and executed the bombing.

The leader of a militia called the Texas Emergency Reserve told a gathering of his members that it was their duty "to purge this land of every nonwhite person, idea, and influence. . . . Enough of this lip service and no action. It's time to begin to train. It is time to begin to reclaim this country for white people."

A Virginia militia's newsletter explained its group's tactics:

> Hit and run tactics will be our method of fighting. . . . We will destroy targets such as telephone relay centers, bridges, fuel storage tanks, communications towers, radio stations, airports. . . . Human targets will be engaged when it is beneficial

A militia member wears his full regalia at a protest rally. Many militia members are dissatisfied with the government.

to the cause to eliminate particular individuals who oppose us (troops, police, political figures . . .).

However, it is not merely the hate-filled messages, posters, and newsletters that are cause for alarm. After all, free speech is a right guaranteed by the Constitution of the United States. "If militias want to be critical of the President, or Jews, or African-Americans, they have the right to do that," explains Jane Bennett, a Chicago attorney interested in the militia movement. "It's when you have people with automatic weapons, grenades, rocket launchers and so on, and who are talking about killing people—wiping out whole groups of people, then it's something very serious, very dangerous. You have that many people with that kind of hate, and the numbers of weapons which they have, and that's a recipe for disaster."

Men are sworn in during a ceremony for new recruits at a militia training site. Many people in law enforcement are worried that such militias may move from voicing dissatisfaction with the government to terroristic acts against it.

"We're an easy target"

Yet many members of citizen militias in the United States reject the idea that they are a threat to anyone's well-being, describing themselves as patriots who are simply misunderstood by an increasingly overbearing government. "Militias didn't bomb anybody," declares John Trochmann of the Militia of Montana. "We're an easy target for the federal government. They'd like to point fingers at us, and accuse us of all sorts of things—that way they have a reason to take our guns away. But it's not going to happen."

"The last hope"

Mark Koernke, spokesman for the Michigan Militia, agrees that militia members are the true patriots. "In many ways we are the last hope this country has before the rights of its people are destroyed," Koernke claims. "The enemy is not the militia, it is the federal government that wants to take our money, take our guns. But be warned . . . we won't surrender what little wealth we have! When the time comes, we *all* have to be in the militias!"

But not all voices of the militia movement are hysterical—many militia members insist that they have no intention of fighting anybody. Their groups, they say, are little more than outdoors-loving civic organizations; they are men who enjoy the camaraderie of an army-type setting. "We like to shoot, take some target practice," says a Minnesota man who belongs to a militia. "What's wrong with that?"

But experts are concerned that there is more to militias than meets the eye. They warn that although some militias do not make racist or terroristic statements publicly, their private agendas are becoming more and more extremist, and that unless Americans pay attention, more tragedies like the Oklahoma City bombing may lie ahead.

1

The Roots of the Militia Movement

THE MILITIA MOVEMENT in the United States gained enormous strength in the mid-1990s and captured a great deal of media attention. But although what are now called militias are only a few years old—none dating before 1990—the movement itself can be traced back many years, all the way to America's beginnings.

"A little rebellion"

At the time of the American Revolution, the word *militia* was in common use. It referred to an army organized and trained at a local level. It was the militias of various colonies that fought the British; indeed, almost every one of the founders associated with America's revolution participated in a local militia.

When the former colonists won their independence and were faced with the task of establishing a nation, they resisted the idea of a powerful federal, or central, government. Having experienced oppression under the control of a remote ruler, the founders and early lawmakers were unwilling to give too much power to any entity more distant than the state government. Should any federal government try to deprive state governments of their powers, many of them believed, it was up to the citizens to rebel. "A little rebellion, now and then, is a good thing," declared Thomas Jefferson, "and as necessary in the political world as storms in the physical."

A volunteer minuteman warns others of the need to grab arms to form a militia. In the early days of the United States, most men protected their families and homes by participating in such militias.

It is easy to see why the prospect of a large standing army under the control of a federal government presented such a threat. What if such an army were used against the states themselves? No, the founders reasoned, it would be far better for the states to organize men into militias. Citizens could not only be called into battle should the United States be threatened by invasion, but also serve as a check against what James Madison termed the "enterprises of ambition" of the federal government.

Losing control of the local militias

In 1792 Congress passed the Militia Act, which required "every free able-bodied white male citizen of the respective states, resident therein, who is or shall be of the age of 18 years and under the age of 45 years" to enroll in a militia. Each enlistee was required to report with a good musket, a bayonet, and twenty-four rounds of ammunition.

Gradually, over the next century, these original militias evolved into scattered units called on to support police in putting down civil disturbances or reacting to natural disasters. In 1903, Congress designated that pool of men in the state militias "the National Guard." Although trained and organized at the state level, the National Guard was officially under the control of the federal government.

Individual states can still establish their own militias, but may not support them with federal funds. In the late twentieth century, there are fewer than twenty-five state militias.

Many state legislators argue that local militias are unnecessary today, and that's why so few states have them. "It's not as though states worry about protecting themselves from the federal government," says one Wisconsin legislator. "And they don't need to fend off attacks from other states. For a natural disaster, such as a flood or an earthquake, we have the services of the Red Cross and the National Guard. I don't think lawmakers would have much success convincing taxpayers that they have to fund a state militia, too."

Roots in hatred?

Some members of citizen militias claim that their organizations are rooted in the eighteenth century, with the patriots and founders. "You read about the incredible bravery of those men," says a Michigan Militia spokesman, "and it makes you so proud to realize where your roots are. That's what being a patriot is about—taking on the whole world if you have to, just to stand up for the Constitution, for all the rights you have been guaranteed."

But while members of citizen militias like to describe themselves as patriots, these militias bear little resemblance to those of Thomas Jefferson's day. Experts say most of the new militias exceed the eighteenth-century militias' distrust of the federal government. The extremist views of today's militias have their foundation in the 1860s, with the creation of the Ku Klux Klan.

The Klan was created in the years just following the Civil War by some former Confederate soldiers in Pulaski, Tennessee. According to its founders, the Klan was for men who

Most experts believe that today's militias share characteristics with the Ku Klux Klan because they dislike the government and show intolerance toward blacks and other minority groups. Here, early Klan members raid the home of a black family.

wanted "to have fun, make mischief, and to play pranks on the public." But the actual activities of the Klan were anything but innocent. The Klan was made up of men outraged that the federal government had not only freed the slaves, but also changed the entire way of life for the South.

Soon after its formation, it was clear that the Ku Klux Klan had a political agenda that vented their anger. Klan activity included nighttime raids that involved the burning of homes, the destruction of farms, and the murder of both freed black slaves and white sympathizers.

The federal government's response to the Klan came in 1871, when President Ulysses S. Grant ordered troops to South Carolina to stop the raids. "Night riding"—the term used to describe the Klan's raids—was made a federal crime.

Hatred against "outsiders"

Although the Klan's activity lessened considerably after postwar reconstruction ended and federal troops were no longer a presence in the South, the organization did not disappear. Quite the contrary—Klan membership skyrocketed during the 1920s, as many black people moved from the South to northern cities after World War I. In 1924 the Klan boasted a membership of 4 million, a large percentage of that in the American Midwest. At that time Klan leader Caleb Ridley remarked, "The first principle of the Klan is that it is a white man's organization. . . . The Klan believes in the supremacy of the Anglo-Saxon race, now and forever. This is a white man's country."

Although the Klan also voiced its objection to the increased presence of Jews and Catholics in the United States, its primary target was black Americans. Klan membership swelled again in the 1950s and 1960s, as desegregation became the law of the land. Sweeping federal legislation requiring that black citizens no longer be treated as second-class citizens infuriated many white southerners. And the Klan was ready to serve as an outlet for that anger.

"Whether in the 1860s or the 1960s, [the Klan] counted on a shared perception that 'outsiders' were trying to change 'the way things were,' leaving local folk with little control over their lives," writes social historian Kenneth Sterns. As that shared perception grew more and more pronounced, violence in the South against civil rights workers and black citizens intensified. Between 1956 and 1966, more than a thousand violent crimes, including beatings, destruction of property, and murder, were attributed to Klan members.

Hate militias in the '30s

A burst of new armed extremist groups that were violently anti-Semitic appeared in the 1930s. Most of these groups were tiny, but several boasted membership in the thousands. One of the most violent was the Silver Shirts, a group that modeled itself after Hitler's storm troopers nicknamed "Brown Shirts." Led by William Dudley Pelley and

Roy Zachary, the Silver Shirts numbered about twenty-five thousand. Most members lived in the western states.

Like any paramilitary group, the Silver Shirts trained regularly for armed confrontation with the federal government. Like many ultraright, or reactionary, groups of the day, the Silver Shirts were critical of Franklin Roosevelt and his New Deal, or "Jew Deal" as they called it. They worried that the relief measures sought by Roosevelt to help the U.S. economy during the depression were little more than communist ideas, which they believed to be the plottings of Jewish financial and business leaders. They believed also that those leaders and their communist supporters controlled the labor unions and the president himself, and that what they saw as the "American Christian way of life" was in jeopardy as a result. Roy Zachary gained na-

Police break up a Silver Shirts meeting in 1938. The Silver Shirts, a violent militia in the 1930s, threatened to assassinate Franklin Roosevelt.

tional attention in 1938 when he announced that if no one else was prepared to assassinate the president, he'd be glad to do it himself.

The Christian Front was another paramilitary hate group of the 1930s. Led by a priest, Father Charles E. Coughlin, the Christian Front was strongly anti-Semitic. As host of a weekly radio show, Coughlin warned his listeners that it was the Jews who started the revolutions in Russia and in Spain, and that they would soon do the same in America. He railed against President Roosevelt, whom he called "President Rosenfeld" (a sarcastic reference to a Jewish-sounding name), calling him an untrustworthy pawn of the wealthy Jews. It was necessary, he said, to arm, train, and organize a Christian Front to do battle against the Jewish Red, or Communist, Front.

Undercover amid terrorists

Much of Coughlin's inflammatory rhetoric was just talk, but in fact a great deal of violence resulted from Christian Front activities. Christian Front members organized attacks not only on Jewish-owned businesses but on Jews themselves, and Coughlin warned that this was just the beginning. A large chapter of the Christian Front in New York City mapped out plans to destroy entire Jewish neighborhoods. Informants reported that the Front was having little trouble assembling an arsenal of weapons; sympathetic sources at Fort Dix, in nearby New Jersey, were supplying ammunition.

Writer Arthur Derounian went undercover among the Christian Front in 1939 and was startled by what he found:

> Some [members] boasted about gun-running activities. One said, "Jew hunting is going to be pretty good soon, and we are practicing." Another predicted "the boys" would "dynamite Detroit, Pittsburgh, Chicago—paralyze transportation and isolate whole sections of the country. . . . A bloodbath is the only way out." One group which paralleled the activities of the Christian Front used the Hitler salute [and] mapped "every arsenal, subway station, power house, police and gasoline station, public building" . . . to prepare for an armed uprising."

Charles E. Coughlin, head of the Christian Front of the 1930s, was strongly anti-Semitic.

Christian identity

Besides the Ku Klux Klan and the extremist anti-Semitic groups of the 1930s, modern militias' roots lie in a religious movement called Christian Identity. This religion, says militia expert Morris Dees, is "the theological thread that binds the diverse . . . segments of the racist movement into a whole cloth." It is very unlike any other Christian denomination; religious historian J. Gordon Melton believes its followers to be full of hate and mentally unstable, when he refers to Christian Identity as "a religion by sociopaths, for sociopaths." Morris Dees labels it "religion on steroids." But most experts agree that to understand the ideas of Christian Identity is to gain a window into the ideas of today's militia movement.

The religion was founded in 1946 by a former Ku Klux Klan organizer from Alabama named Wesley Swift. Swift was an avowed racist who believed that members of the white race, whom he referred to as "Aryans," were the true chosen people of the Old Testament. The Jews, on the other hand, were the offspring of Satan, and were by their very nature evil. For Christians to hate Jews, say Swift's followers, is not an emotional or personal choice, but a necessary reaction of good to evil.

"There are no words in the English language, or any other, to adequately describe a Jew," states Thomas O'Brien, a leader of the modern Christian Identity Church. "You cannot, hard as you may try, insult a Jew, because the very vilest and foulest things you can think of to say about him, are nothing but pure and unadulterated flattery in comparison to what he really is."

Blacks, Asians, and other nonwhites are called "mud people" by Christian Identity believers. According to their interpretation of the Bible, God created "mud people" sometime between the creation of animals and Adam and Eve, the perfect, white human beings. To call "mud people" human, or to treat them with the same respect one would accord human beings, says one Christian Identity minister, is to miss the whole point.

"Children are little people, little human beings, and that means white people. . . . There's little dogs and cats and apes and baboons and skunks and there's also little niggers. But they ain't children. They're just little niggers."

The militant Jesus

Pastor Pete Peters, the most often quoted of Christian Identity leaders, laughs when other Christians are shocked by the anti-Semitic, racist teachings of his church. Other Christian denominations, he says, are examples of "refined, goody-goody religion that . . . is tenderly embraced by an effeminate [female] world." True Christianity, he preaches, is not gentle and loving. He points to Bible verses in which Jesus tells his disciples to arm themselves with swords, even if they have to sell their garments to do so. Peters says that the sword in Jesus' day was the equivalent of an M-16 today, and it is the duty of every Christian "not only to own one, but be able to use one."

The need for weapons, according to Christian Identity, is based on the belief that race war is imminent between whites and nonwhites, the latter including what Christian Identity believers call "the race traitors"—whites who marry outside their own race.

"This war we call Armageddon, and it will be a time when white people must be brave," declares one Christian Identity spokesman. "The faithful are even today taking up weapons and have put away food and provisions for that day. We know the enemies, and when the time comes, God will command that blacks, Asians, Jews, homosexuals, race traitors, and others will be put to death."

The Posse Comitatus

From the violent teachings of Christian Identity an extremist group called the Posse Comitatus was born in the late 1960s, becoming especially active in the 1980s. One of its first leaders, William Potter Gale, had been one of the early leaders of the Christian Identity movement. Gale believed that the problems faced by modern society were the result of improper, illegitimate governments. According to Gale, any government higher than the county level is illegitimate, and therefore evil. (The name Posse Comitatus is Latin for "the power of the county.") The highest court in the land is that of the county, and the sheriff the highest elected official, according to Posse Comitatus doctrine. Like Christian Identity, Posse Comitatus members believed that Jews and nonwhites controlled the federal government, with the goal of taking over power and jobs from Aryans.

Like many of today's militias, Posse Comitatus considered itself as a collection of patriots, much like those of the American Revolution. As Benjamin Franklin, Thomas Jefferson, and Samuel Adams had declared taxation illegal, so did the leaders of Posse Comitatus. Posse leaders tried to convince others to stop paying taxes altogether.

Like Christian Identity and other extremist groups, Posse Comitatus urged action against its enemies. Members sent death threats to local and state officials who they believed were acting in violation of the Constitution. The group also prided itself on its stockpile of sophisticated weapons, to be used against either agents of the federal or state government who took action against Posse Comitatus or against Jews, blacks, or other nonwhites. Adherents were convinced that a race war on American soil was inevitable, and that God had ordained that the Aryans would win.

"Yes, we are going to cleanse our land [of nonwhites]," declared Gale in a 1989 radio broadcast. "We're going to do it with a sword. And we're going to do it with violence. You're damn right I'm teaching violence. God said you're going to do it that way, and it's about time somebody is telling you to get violent, whitey."

Law enforcement officials in the 1980s took the organization seriously. "The symbol of the group was always a hangman's noose," remembers one South Dakota sheriff's department employee. "They said that they had the authority to hang anybody who takes away their freedoms, whether it's making them register their guns, or even making them pay income tax. Some of them wear a little noose on their lapel, like some people would wear a Lion's Club pin or an AIDS ribbon or something."

Taking on the government

Rather than deny their group's willingness to resort to violence, Posse members were proud of their willingness to stand up for their principles, in the manner of the patriots of the Revolution. Their handbook stressed that any citizen has a constitutional right to arm himself and defend himself against thieves, in which category they place Internal Revenue Service agents. Any government official who threatens citizens by "stealing" from them, says the handbook, "shall be removed by the Posse . . . and at high noon be hung by the neck, the body remaining until sundown as an example to those who would subvert the law."

Probably the most famous of Posse Comitatus members was Gordon Kahl, who became a martyr for the organization's cause in 1983. Kahl, a North Dakota farmer, had been a vocal critic of the income tax code in the United States for many years. He scoffed at the notion that the federal or state government had the power to tax him or his land. Like many other Posse Comitatus members, he also refused to hold a driver's license or buy license plates for his truck.

Kahl was convicted of tax evasion in 1977 and sentenced to a year in prison and five years' probation. However, when he was released from prison, he refused to honor either his tax debt or his probation agreement. On February 13, 1983, federal authorities attempted to arrest Kahl. In the gun battle that followed, Kahl shot and killed two sheriff's deputies and wounded two other officers. He escaped and was a fugitive for several months, staying at his Arkansas hideout. Late in 1983, he was killed in a gun battle with federal agents. Kahl's death made him a hero in the eyes of many white supremacists and Christian Identity believers. He was viewed as a patriot who had died at the hands of the federal government. He had died for his beliefs, and that made his cause seem that much more noble, and the government that much more hostile and unreasonable. Hundreds of people attended his funeral to hear him praised as a "God-fearing, gun-toting patriot, a brave and dedicated soldier for the cause."

The Order

If Gordon Kahl's death provided the extremists with a martyr for their cause, neo-Nazi leader William Pierce provided them with an important piece of literature—some say a blueprint for future militia violence.

In 1978, using the pen name Andrew Macdonald, Pierce wrote *The Turner Diaries*, a fictitious account of a militia called the Order. Angered by what they believed was a Jewish-controlled federal government that was taking away their freedoms one by one, the Order plotted and carried out acts of terrorism.

Pierce presented the book as a sort of step-by-step guidebook for those who believe, as he did, that "we are engaged in the most desperate war we have ever fought. A war for the survival of our race. . . . Ultimately we cannot win it except by killing our enemies." Pierce himself was very explicit in naming the enemies who will be killed:

> All the homosexuals, race mixers, and hard-case collaborators in the country who are too far gone to be reeducated can be rounded up, packed in 10,000 or so railroad cattle cars, and eventually double-timed into an abandoned coal mine in a few days time.

Pierce's book went on sale strictly through mail-order, not bookstores. Even with such limited distribution, more than 200,000 copies were sold. It is not known how many of his readers believed as strongly as he did in his principles of hate. However, the book did spawn an ultrasecret militia. Also calling itself "the Order," the forty-man organization went on a spree of bloodshed and destruction between 1983 and 1984.

A real-life Order

Its leader, an anti-Semite and white supremacist named Robert Mathews, closely modeled his little army on the Order in Pierce's book. A month after Gordon Kahl's death in June 1983, Mathews and his organization began seeking ways to finance their operation. Like the militia in Pierce's book, they attempted counterfeiting fifty-dollar bills, but their printing presses could not produce bills that appeared genuine enough to circulate without drawing suspicion.

They turned to robbery, holding up a series of banks and armored cars along the West Coast that netted more than $4 million. According to the Southern Poverty Law Center, a watchdog group that monitors extremist organizations in the United States, the money was distributed to white supremacists and Nazi groups around the country. Some federal sources claimed Mathews had sent a sizable amount to Pierce, as thanks for writing his book, although Pierce has denied receiving money from the Order.

However, robbery was only a portion of the Order's activity. Members bombed synagogues and sent threatening mail to prominent Jews and African Americans. They stockpiled weapons and planned the destruction of dams, bridges, and even federal buildings—the idea being to throw the U.S. public into confusion and panic. They murdered individuals they considered enemies, among them Alan Berg, a Jewish radio talk-show host who had been openly critical of the Order.

The group dissolved after Mathews was killed in a shootout with FBI agents in Puget Sound, Washington, in December 1994. Other members were eventually appre-

hended and tried on charges including counterfeiting, armed robbery, conspiracy, and murder. All were sentenced to lengthy prison terms.

What was the reaction of William Pierce, whose book was Mathews's blueprint for race war? He had nothing but kind words for the real-life Order after Mathews's death. "Bob gave us a very important symbol," said Pierce. "He did what was morally right. . . . He took us from name calling to bloodletting. He cleared the air for all. In the long run, that will be helpful."

Whether or not he knew it at the time, Pierce's words were all too prophetic. The bloodletting, begun by a handful of small extremist groups, would increase mightily within only a few years.

2

The Cornerstones
of Today's Militias

UNTIL 1993 THE EXTREMISTS of the far right were fragmented and disorganized. Most belonged to organizations that advocated violence; often, however, they had little else in common. Their anger was rooted in various issues. Some, like the Klan, targeted blacks. Others were incited more by what they perceived as the strong control Jews had over the federal government. Some, like the believers in Christian Identity, had a political agenda based on their interpretation of the Bible. Other agendas focused on what was considered a corrupt economic system, opposing the income tax and banking practices.

"In simple terms, it was a disagreement over who should be shot," says one sociologist. "Should it be the Latinos and the blacks, or the gays and the race mixers? Or should they just declare war on the federal government and be done with it? There was certainly nothing that bound the various groups other than hatred."

Two events—the first in late summer of 1992 and the second in the spring of 1993—changed this situation. The first event gave the various hate groups a common cause, a focus for their hatred. It was, as Morris Dees writes in *Gathering Storm: America's Militia Threat*, an event "that sparked the militia movement and set into motion the chain of events that is still unfolding." Six months later the second event fanned that spark into a roaring fire.

Ruby Ridge

Randy Weaver is a thin, hollow-eyed veteran, a former Green Beret who fought in Vietnam. He and his wife, Vicki, had three children when they moved from Iowa to a remote wooded area in northern Idaho called Ruby Ridge in the early 1980s. Weaver told people that he had made the move for a couple of reasons. He and Vicki wanted to home school their children, and home schooling regulations were far less strict in Idaho than they were in Iowa. More importantly, their Christian Identity religion encouraged separation from mainstream American society, believed to be evil and corrupt.

Weaver and his wife taught their children the message of Christian Identity—that the government, the media, and the

Militia member Randy Weaver with lawyer Gerry Spence at a Senate committee hearing regarding the FBI raid on Weaver's property in Ruby Ridge, Idaho.

economy of the United States were controlled by Jews, who were descendants of Satan. They told them that the Jews were after one thing: to enslave all white Christians. The Weavers referred to the federal government as ZOG, short for "Zionist Occupied Government" (Zionist being a reference to the movement to reestablish a Jewish homeland in Israel). One of Weaver's favorite T-shirts was imprinted with the white-lettered slogan "Just Say No to ZOG."

Weaver's neighbors near Ruby Ridge remember him as friendly and helpful, although intense about his religious beliefs. "Everything he said started with a quote from the Bible," one man recalls. "He'd say that the end of the world was coming soon, and he wanted to be worthy, so that he'd go to heaven."

A warrant unheeded

Like other Christian Identity believers, Weaver had stockpiled guns and ammunition for the race war which he believed was coming soon. He was approached in January 1991 by a man who said he was part of a neo-Nazi group, and who wanted to buy two sawed-off shotguns. Weaver sold him the weapons and found himself under arrest; the neo-Nazi turned out to be an informant for the federal Bureau of Alcohol, Tobacco, and Firearms (ATF), which ran the sting to arrest white supremacists who were thought to be running an illegal gun business in northern Idaho.

After his arrest, Weaver was released without bail; the judge felt that Weaver's good standing in the community would guarantee that he would show up for his court date the next month. However, Weaver, furious that he had been caught, vowed to shoot anyone who tried to take him into custody. Vicki wrote a scathing letter to federal authorities, telling them, "My husband was set up for a fall because of his religious and political beliefs. There is nothing to discuss. He doesn't have to prove he is innocent. Nor refute your slander."

What Weaver intended to do was to remain with his family atop Ruby Ridge, in his small plywood cabin. Conditions were rather primitive; there was no indoor plumb-

Weaver's primitive cabin after the police raid. Many people believe that the FBI used excessive force in the raid, as both Weaver's wife and teenage son were killed by agents.

ing, no running water, and the only electricity was supplied by a portable generator. Friends and neighbors took turns delivering food, supplies, and the Weavers' mail. When people urged him to turn himself in and tell his side of the story, Weaver refused. He was convinced he could never get a fair trial from the federal government. He declared he would rather die in his cabin than give in. "Even if we die, we win," he said. "We'll die believing in Yahweh [the word he used for God]."

Confrontation

U.S. marshals were reluctant to force Weaver's hand. They knew there were children in the cabin—four now, as

Vicki had given birth to another little girl, Elisheba, since the family went into hiding. Unwilling to risk shooting a child, marshals prudently waited until Weaver was ready to talk.

Authorities kept the vigil in the woods below the Weavers' cabin. Eighteen months went by with no progress in establishing a dialogue. On August 21, 1992, the "wait and see" plan of the U.S. marshals unraveled.

To this day, it is not known exactly who began the shooting; Weaver's and the marshals' accounts differ. It is known that six federal marshals dressed in camouflage gear were monitoring the cabin at 2:30 that morning. A car drove into the valley, and it appeared that Weaver, his fourteen-year-old son Sam, and a family friend named Kevin Harris came out of the cabin to investigate. Their dogs ran before them, dashing down the hill and apparently catching the scent of the marshals.

One of the marshals testified later that he was afraid one of the barking dogs would give their position away, and so shot the dog. Sam and Harris yelled at the man, and then shot at him. An exchange of gunfire began, and a marshal and Sam Weaver were killed—Sam shot in the back as he tried to run back toward his father.

The following day an FBI sharpshooter aiming at Harris shot Vicki, her baby in her arms, as she opened the cabin's front door. She was struck in the head and killed instantly. (Although many militia members believe her death was intentional, FBI spokesmen have called it "accidental.") Harris and Weaver were both wounded, as well. Even so, his wife and son dead, Weaver was more resolved than ever that he would not come down alive. The surveillance had escalated into a shootout.

Support on the road

Marshals and FBI agents set up a barricade on the road leading to the Weavers' cabin. News of the shootings spread throughout the little community, and before long people gathered across the road, taunting the law enforcement agents with signs reading "Leave the Family Alone—

Go Home," "FBI Burn in Hell," "Zionist Murderers," and "Baby Killers."

Not all Weaver's supporters agreed completely with his ideas. "He doesn't like black people," said one, "and his religion is kind of funny, but that's no reason to go after him, to be shooting at his family." Another said, "Randy Weaver just wanted to be left alone, but the government went after his property, his firearms, and now they're paying for it. That man, Randy Weaver, is a patriot, not a criminal."

In the next few days, the crowd at the roadblock grew to include newspaper reporters from across the country and extremists from Christian Identity and the neo-Nazi Aryan Nations. Some came to shout insults at the FBI agents; others brought weapons and ammunition, an illegal act for which five of them were arrested. One neo-Nazi who was arrested told a reporter, "I'm ready to get my gun and my clips and take off my safety and pull my trigger with my finger. I don't care anymore. This is the beginning of a revolution."

Negotiation and surrender

Inside Weaver's cabin, things were falling apart. Five days had gone by since Vicki was shot, and her decomposing body lay under the kitchen table in a deep pool of blood. The baby screamed and cried for her mother. Weaver and his older daughters tried to care for the little girl as well as nurse Harris, whose wounds were rapidly becoming seriously infected.

On Wednesday, August 26, a retired army lieutenant colonel named James "Bo" Gritz approached the authorities at Ruby Ridge. He had served in the Green Berets with Weaver years before, and now volunteered to approach and establish a dialogue with him. Like Weaver, Gritz was a racist and an anti-Semite; in fact, he was running for president in 1992 as the candidate of the extremist Populist Party. "I know Randy," he said, "and I know his Identity religion." FBI agents were reluctant to allow another extremist access to the Ruby Ridge cabin, but two

As the siege of Randy Weaver's cabin dragged on, a former comrade, James "Bo" Gritz (right), volunteered to speak to Weaver. With the help of Gritz, Weaver finally surrendered on August 29, 1992.

days later they permitted Gritz and an associate named Jack McLamb to meet with Weaver.

Three days later, Weaver surrendered to Gritz and McLamb. "He cried his wife's name, he cried his son's name, and then we marched down the road like we said we were going to do," said Gritz. The long ordeal at Ruby Ridge was over. Weaver and Harris were charged with the murder of the federal marshal, and were both taken to the hospital. Gritz, jubilant that his negotiations had worked, gave the neo-Nazis and skinheads along the road a straight-armed Nazi salute as he walked by.

Reactions to Ruby Ridge

For mainstream America, the drama that was played out in northern Idaho sparked no lasting indignation. Weaver, after all, was not a completely innocent victim. As author Morris Dees points out, "Didn't Weaver bring this tragedy down upon himself? Wasn't he a person who believed Jews were the children of Satan? Wasn't he a man wanted for selling sawed-off shotguns? Wasn't a deputy marshal also killed?" Although some who read the news accounts felt sympathy for a man who had lost his wife and young son, it was hard to feel sorry for a man who had remarked that he hoped the shotguns would be sold to black gang members who would then shoot each other.

But the Ruby Ridge incident struck a nerve in some Americans, and Rev. Pete Peters, the head of the Christian Identity Church, sensed that. Peters had written letters of support to Weaver during the standoff; now he believed the time was right to get various right-wing groups—some violent, some not—to unite.

He hoped to persuade the leaders of these various groups to gather in Estes Park, Colorado, to affirm a common purpose. Especially important, he felt, was to tap into the 5-million-strong Patriot movement, which included nonviolent conservative groups such as followers of televangelist Pat Robertson, members of the ultraconservative John Birch Society, and gun owners nervous about proposed government restrictions on their weapons. As Peters said, these were people who "in the past would normally not be caught together under one roof"—either because they viewed each other as adversaries, or because some of the individuals preferred to be viewed as conservative rather than extremist. Relative moderates didn't want their good standing in mainstream communities to be compromised by an association with the more violent right-wing groups such as Christian Identity, the Klan, or Aryan Nations.

An increase in militia membership

In the end Peters persuaded 160 white Christian men from a variety of right-wing organizations to attend the meeting on October 22, 1992. Peters spoke, furious at what he called "a conspiracy on both the part of the media and government." After all, he said, the media "on a national scale, gave little reporting on the murder of this white child and his white mother in comparison to [the attention given] the beating of the black man, Rodney King."

Many of those attending the meeting agreed that the government—by its actions—had increased the membership in extremist organizations. People who ordinarily would not have been joiners were appalled by the killing of Vicki and Sam Weaver, and by what they saw as the harassment of the family by the FBI and U.S. marshals. "All of us in our groups . . . could not have done in the next twenty years what the federals did for our cause in eleven days in . . . Idaho," said Chris Temple, a writer for a Christian Identity newspaper.

During the course of the three-day meeting, some important proposals were adopted. Larry Pratt, head of Gun Owners of America, argued for a "national struggle for survival" with "armed militia units." Another speaker, a leader of Aryan Nations and former Grand Wizard of the Texas Ku Klux Klan named Louis Beam, agreed with Pratt's plan to organize militias. Beam stressed the need for all like-minded organizations to work together, to share resources, mailing lists, and information.

Former Grand Wizard of the Texas Ku Klux Klan, Louis Beam.

Militias and leaderless cells

In addition, Beam proposed a way for the militias to organize and at the same time minimize their risk of detection by law enforcement agencies. He called it "leaderless resistance"—a legal aboveground political group fronting underground illegal activities. It was important, he said, that the militias have no single, central chain of command, as discovery of one segment of a militia could lead to exposure of the entire organization. He called his structure "phantom cell." Each group, made up of between eight and ten members, would operate independently of all others. "Participants in a program of leaderless resistance through phantom cell or individual action must know exactly what they are doing," he instructed, "and exactly how to do it."

As did many speakers, Beam warned his audience that an attack like that on the Weaver family could happen to any family in the United States. "This time the federal terrorists, masquerading as officers, came for Randy Weaver," he said. "Next time they may come for you. . . . If federal terrorism goes unchallenged, then no one in this nation is safe. . . . Like a lion having tasted the blood of human victims, they will come for more, new victims."

There was tumultuous cheering and applause when Beam and Peters called for the new militias to avenge the deaths of Vicki and Sam Weaver. There is no doubt that the October 1992 meeting in Estes Park laid the groundwork for the modern militia movement. Only six months later a second event would give the movement just the impetus it needed to explode onto the American scene.

Preparing for the end of the world

The event, like that at Ruby Ridge, has become known by the name of the place where it occurred—Waco, Texas. And like the standoff between the government and the Weavers, Waco has been made a symbol of unfettered government brutality, resulting in the deaths of, among others, innocent children.

The government's opponent in Waco was a cult called the Branch Davidians, a breakaway sect of Seventh Day Adventists. They believed strongly in the need to prepare for doomsday, the end of the world at which time God would come down from heaven to assist the faithful in their struggle with the "evil" government. Preparing for this apocalypse required the Branch Davidians to stockpile automatic weapons, a great store of ammunition, and grenades.

The Branch Davidian compound in Waco, Texas.

The professed leader of the group was David Koresh, a charismatic, forceful thirty-three-year-old. He claimed that he alone could translate secret messages from the Book of Revelation and interpret their meaning. And their meaning, according to Koresh, was very clear: The Branch Davidians must assemble as many weapons and as much ammunition as possible, for the end was coming soon. In May 1992, forty thousand dollars' worth of guns, gun parts, chemicals, fuses, grenades, and ammunition was delivered to their isolated compound. During shipment, a box broke open, revealing the contents. The UPS delivery driver alerted the local sheriff, who in turn notified the FBI and ATF.

ATF kept a close watch on the Davidians' comings and goings, and later devised a secret plan to raid the Branch Davidian compound on February 28, 1993. Koresh got word of the plan somehow, and stated very matter-of-factly, "Neither the ATF nor the National Guard will ever get me."

A fiery inferno

Even without the element of surprise, the ATF decided to carry out the scheduled raid. Seventy armed ATF agents stormed the compound. A shootout ensued; four ATF agents were killed, many others wounded. In addition, seven Davidians were killed, including Koresh's two-year-old daughter.

For the next fifty-one days, federal agents took up positions outside the compound. They were prepared, they said, to wait Koresh out. They wanted no more scenes like Ruby Ridge or the confrontation in which Gordon Kahl of the Posse Comitatus was killed. Patience would be the order of the day. Meanwhile, FBI agents negotiated for the release of twenty-three people from the compound, many of them children.

An ATF officer watches the Koresh compound in March 1993.

Outside the compound, federal officers were waging psychological warfare, trying to draw the rest of the Davidians out. They cut off the cult's electricity. All day and all night they blasted Christmas carols, loud sirens, Tibetan chants, and the sounds of rabbits being slaughtered over huge speakers aimed at the compound. But it was the federal agents whose resolve wore down first. With the authorization of Attorney General Janet Reno, the FBI decided to approach the buildings in tanks on April 19, using tear gas to force Koresh and his followers out.

The FBI's decision was a foolish one, as many agents now concede. It underestimated Koresh and his followers' fanaticism and their willingness to die for their beliefs. Within a few minutes of the release of the gas, fire erupted from inside the compound. Strong winds soon turned the city-block-size building into an inferno. Although fire trucks were summoned, the FBI kept them away, fearing

ATF agents cover their faces to guard against the cold during the standoff in Waco. Hoping to wait the Branch Davidians out, the agents later became restless and stormed the compound.

the firefighters would be shot. In the end Koresh and eighty of his followers died in the fire. Twenty-four victims were children.

A reaction of horror

The raid on the Branch Davidians was televised, and many Americans looked on in shock and horror. The source of the fire was unclear; no one could say if federal agents or the Davidians themselves had set it, deliberately or accidentally. But no matter how the fire started, people asked themselves why the FBI was so eager to storm the compound.

There were many, too, who had no questions at all. These were members of the Patriot movement who were not surprised by what they called "the intentional brutality and violence of the federal government." Hadn't this happened before, at Ruby Ridge?

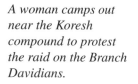

A woman camps out near the Koresh compound to protest the raid on the Branch Davidians.

Reactions from the far right were harsh. One member of a neo-Nazi group said, "The Waco Church Holocaust, in which many worshipers, including innocent children, were burned alive while worshiping in their church, was an atrocity which surpasses the worst accusations made against the Nazis in Germany."

So the anger felt by the right wing and the Patriot movement toward the federal government increased. At Ruby Ridge the anger built. But at Waco, the anger turned to rage and distrust, until it seemed to those who monitored right-wing activity that the situation was dangerously volatile. A militia member from Florida claimed later, "Waco awakened the whole [movement]. That put the fear of God into us."

3

Conspiracies and Paranoia

HATRED AND DISTRUST of the federal government has not subsided among the militias and other extremist groups in America since the Waco and Ruby Ridge incidents. If anything, such emotions have intensified, in part due to recent legislation such as the Brady Bill, which imposes a mandatory five-day waiting period on the purchase of handguns.

"There's no question—or there shouldn't be in anybody's eyes," declares a member of the Florida Militia,

> ZOG is out to get us, get our guns, get our ammunition. We know without a doubt that foreign troops who are going to help the federal government are at this very moment massing their troops in various secret places throughout this country. It'll just be a matter of time. And we know that, because the government is evil—it's trying to establish the New World Order. And you see, it's up to the righteous to stand against it.

A different slant on history

To Americans not affiliated with the far right, many of these claims about government conspiracies seem paranoid if not delusional. "They are nervous that they are being spied on by black helicopters, they think the government has ordered doctors to put tiny microchip scanners under the skin of newborn babies, and they think the UN [United Nations] armies are ready to take over America by force," says one sociologist who studies militia behavior. "They are convinced—not only that these things are possible—but that they are true, and are taking place right now."

Such beliefs, say experts, fit what political historian Richard Hofstadter defined in 1965 as "the paranoid view of history." Throughout history, says Hofstadter, various groups of people have believed that there is a central machine—in this case, the federal government—that is inherently evil and bent on destroying them. This mind-set leads to an "us versus them" extremism. Says Hofstadter:

> [They see] history . . . as a conspiracy, set in motion by demonic forces of almost transcendent power, and what is felt to be needed to defeat it is not the usual methods of political give-and-take, but an all-out crusade. The paranoid spokesman sees the fate of his conspiracy in apocalyptic terms. . . . Time is forever just running out. . . . He does not see social conflict as something to be mediated and compromised. . . . Since what is at stake is always a conflict between absolute good and absolute evil, the quality needed is not a willingness to compromise but the will to fight things out to the finish.

"Careful, men! The government has made the weather gorgeous today so we'd let our guard down. They can't fool us . . . they're coming for our guns!"

The New World Order

One of the foremost conspiracy themes in the militia movement is that of the New World Order. It is what far-right militants fear most—the establishment of a world community in which American independence is lost forever. In their eyes, says militia expert Richard Abanes, "most Americans are [blithely] marching into a . . . global community wherein all international borders and national sovereignty will be destroyed. The coming . . . regime allegedly will reduce humanity to slaves, whose sole purpose will be to serve the international [Jewish] bankers, wealthy elite, socialists, and liberals."

The phrase "new world order" was first used by political commentators in the late 1980s in connection with the fall of communism in Eastern Europe and dismantling of the Soviet Union. For some, says militia expert Thomas Halpern, "it embodied hope, now that the Cold War was over, for a spirit of cooperation in international relations and problem-solving." However, Halpern says, the term was given a very different spin by extremists who see the New World Order as a shadowy, sinister conspiracy between the federal government and the United Nations to merge the nations of the world into one government.

President Bush and the New World Order

During the 1990–1991 Persian Gulf crisis, President George Bush unknowingly played into conspiracy theorists' hands. In a speech before Congress on September 11, 1990, Bush stated:

> We stand today at a unique and extraordinary moment. . . . Out of these troubled times . . . a new world order can emerge; a new era—free from the threat of terror, stronger in the pursuit of justice, and more secure in the quest for peace, an era in which the nations of the world, East and West, North and South, can prosper and live in harmony.

According to presidential aides, Bush was referring to a sort of renewal of the original purpose of the United Nations, that is, to promote peace and negotiate problems between countries. The speech went on to express hope that

When George Bush innocently gave a speech that included a reference to "the beginning of a new world order," he was unaware that these words would panic militia movements across the nation.

the time was right for UN members to usher in an era "where diverse nations are drawn together in common cause."

Yet, says Halpern, Bush's reference to "the beginning of a new world order" was a bombshell among far-right extremists. "What stuck in the minds of many militia proponents was a vision of the subordination of the United States to an international collective, resulting in the surrender of its national sovereignty and the stripping away of the freedoms that Americans enjoy."

An inside job

But how could such a monumental takeover occur? Militia leaders believe it will occur with the help of the federal government and all of the agencies upon which Americans depend for law and order. And the center of the massive conspiracy, says Michigan Militia leader Mark Koernke, is a Multi-Jurisdictional Task Force (MJTF)—a kind of national police force. This force is being created as what he calls "the umbrella group that will make up the national police force in the United States." According to Koernke, the MJTF will disarm Americans who own weapons, put militia members and other rebels in concentration camps that are being built throughout America by another of the agencies militias fear most, the Federal Emergency Management Agency (FEMA). FEMA was organized in 1978 by President Jimmy Carter; its purpose was to plan for emergencies, natural or human-made, nuclear disasters in particular. In case of nuclear war, Carter decided, FEMA could be a back up system if the federal government was destroyed.

When the Soviet Union's government collapsed, however, the role of FEMA was redefined to that of disaster relief in the event of earthquakes, tornadoes, and so on. However, many militia members are suspicious of FEMA's stated purpose. "We have the Red Cross, we have the National Guard," says one member of a California militia. "Why in the world do we need FEMA—tell me that? The answer is, no we don't need it at all."

Concentration camps in the United States?

The agency's real purpose, according to militia leaders, is twofold. First, it is supposed to wage a campaign of terror, getting more weapons into the hands of Los Angeles and Chicago street gangs, so they can serve as muscle for leaders of the New World Order. FEMA's second purpose is to operate as a "shadow government" that will assume control once the old government topples. As one extremist newsletter warned in 1994, "When the federal government decides to enact martial law; and they will; the Director of FEMA becomes a virtual DICTATOR. . . . The American people will be held in bondage and be killed on the spot with impunity; even if they are in the right."

According to militia leaders, thousands of Americans will be herded into concentration camps, where they will be either enslaved or killed. The Wolverine Brigade of the Southern Michigan Regional Militia claims that a network of crematoriums (for disposing of the bodies) and concentration camps has already been established for this purpose.

Such concentration camps are nonexistent, say officials at FEMA and the FBI. What militia members have observed are merely fenced-off storage areas, they explain.

Enemy troops now on American soil?

Because most right-wing extremists and militia members tend to cut themselves off from the rest of society and to develop their beliefs only among a circle of like-minded fellows, the New World Order conspiracy theory has thrived, and been embellished with additional detail.

For instance, it is a common belief among militias that foreign and UN troops are not only going to take over America but actually already are assembled on American soil, waiting for the right moment to attack. Some militia members report that there are UN troops hiding under-

ground in specially constructed bunkers in Detroit, in remote areas of Mississippi, and even in submarines off the
coast of California.

John Trochmann, head of the relatively high-profile
Militia of Montana, says that such troops are simply waiting for the order to attack, and that when they do, Americans will be overwhelmed. "When the troops come in,
they'll come in with such force it will be incredible!" he
exclaims. "In 48 hours, they can have 100 million troops

*Militia groups protest
outside the United
Nations. Many militias
fear and despise the
UN, believing that the
organization will result
in the eventual
subjugation of the
United States.*

here. They'll come out of the ground! They'll come from submarines! . . . They'll come from everywhere!"

Militia members report numerous sightings of these attack forces, especially in the West and Northwest. For instance, one militia spokesperson wrote of "black-suited, unidentified ninja-types doing 'practice runs' in Alaska, pulling citizens over, demanding an ID, searching their cars, then letting them go, while refusing to provide ID themselves and holding the citizens at gunpoint in the process, occurring in Alaska."

Blue helmets and Russians at the Chicken Lickin'

Another militia—this one in northern California—spotted a group of men wearing blue helmets rappelling from an unidentified helicopter behind a government building. The militia members immediately concluded that these were the UN New World Order troops, and that the takeover had begun. As the militia considered launching an armed attack, one member decided to ask about the strange goings-on. He was assured that the men were not UN troops, but smoke jumpers (forest firefighters) in training.

The militia was unconvinced by this answer, however. The rumor about UN troops in the northern California forest was repeated to members of other militias, and soon word of the UN's "secret training operation" had spread throughout the country through Patriot newspapers, short-wave radio communications, and Internet postings.

Elsewhere, a popular anti-Semitic newspaper called the *Spotlight* reported that Russian troops were massing in the deserts of Arizona. As evidence, it cited reports of disabled Russian vehicles along a road and a half-dozen Russian soldiers eating at a nearby restaurant called the Chicken Lickin'.

It was suspicious, the newspaper article went on, "that the soldiers, when approached by curious customers and employees of the restaurant, indicated that they were Americans training as OPFORS (opposing forces) . . . at [a nearby army] base." However, as writer Kenneth Stern

A militia member attends a training weekend that gathered members from several states.

writes, "The *Spotlight* apparently was not bothered by the illogic that secret Russian invaders—who presumably would not want to draw attention to themselves—would risk all by a meal at the Chicken Lickin'." Stern further asks, "And did the *Spotlight* think about the fact that these gentlemen spoke English?"

"They add 2 and 2 and come up with 10"

More and more rumors circulate, often based on sightings of unusual or unidentifiable uniforms or equipment. "The thing is, a lot of these rumors are founded on something real—like a real sighting of something," says one militia expert.

> And so there is just enough information to ring true; maybe a bunch of people saw the same thing. And they start talking, and theorizing about what they've seen, and pretty soon they're all convinced it was part of the New World Order. It's as though they add 2 and 2 and come up with 10.

Robert Brown, publisher of *Soldier of Fortune* magazine, agrees. "What these people do," he says, "is take certain pieces of information, selectively interpret them, put them together, and the whole becomes much greater than the sum [of the parts]."

Although many of the so-called "paranoid conspiracy theories" have some basis in fact, militia members put their own spin on the information, say militia experts. And those who believe in the idea of a New World Order conspiracy can often find what they feel are sure signs of that conspiracy.

For example, many militia and Patriot organizations think that the coded bars on the backs of many road signs are directions for incoming New World Order troops. "Even if they can't read English," says a Florida Patriot, "those codes can guide them to the concentration camp, to water or fuel depots—whatever."

Transportation officials, debunking this rumor, say these codes merely contain information about the date and maker of the signs. "I can assure you that these are not for invading troops," states a spokesman for the Michigan Department of Transportation.

Black helicopters

There is probably no more widely reported sign of the New World Order conspiracy than the sightings of black, unmarked helicopters, mostly in the western United States. According to Jim Keith, author of the book *Black Helicopters over America: Strikeforce for the New World Order*, the helicopters are "flying over our land in violation of all local and federal laws, carrying out their secret business, and taunting and terrifying the populace."

Most militia members suspect these craft are owned and operated by FEMA or UN troops, and are being used to gather information about Patriots. The helicopters have also been blamed for many unexplained events. Says Keith, "The first documented sightings were in 1971, in Lake County, Colorado, when 40 sheep were found dead and 'blistered' in some unknown manner, after a rancher observed a helicopter flying over the animals."

The magazine *Spotlight* has also reported sightings and mysterious things that coincidently occur when the black helicopters are sighted. One story says that the ghostly helicopters "have been chasing people, hovering over houses, following cars on the roads, killing birds and cattle, and pointing what appeared to be guns at people."

Explanations are not enough

These stories, however, present a basic problem for individuals attempting to check their validity. As Abanes states, "The bulk of these accounts come from anonymous witnesses whose stories cannot be verified. Witnesses include 'girls on horseback'; 'two girls out walking'; 'a family'; 'a man driving a pickup truck'; 'a rancher'; 'a state trooper'; 'a hunter.'"

This does not mean that the accounts are false, however. Experts have been asked to offer explanations for what appear to be unmarked black helicopters. Major Tom Schultz of the Colorado National Guard says that such helicopters do exist, although they are not the ominous craft militias suspect are ushering in the New World Order. Schultz explains that over the last few years many green military helicopters have been treated with a special coating that makes them chemical resistant. They *are* dark, with black lettering, and Shultz freely admits that "they may appear black and unmarked to casual observers because anyone further than 100 yards from the aircraft is not going to see the markings."

Various sources state that the dark helicopters are used for training exercises, to search for poachers and lost or missing persons, and even to investigate reports of remote marijuana cultivation. The military denies that soldiers threaten citizens with guns or that helicopters have killed animals.

But the militias are not swayed by such explanations and denials. "We know what we see," says a Nevada Militia commander. "And what we see scares us, and should scare anyone who loves this country and its constitution. The invasion of the New World Order is on the horizon. If people

want to laugh and call us crazy, let 'em. But we won't go down without a fight."

"Biochips" and clues on money

As adamant as the majority of militia members are about black helicopters and the New World Order, however, other theories seem wildly far-fetched and prompt doubts even among some militia members.

One such theory advanced by the Militia of Montana maintains that a map of the United States taken from the back of a box of Kix cereal in 1993 is actually a representation of the New World Order's plan to divide up the country into separate regions. Another rumor claims that "biochips" are being surgically inserted under the skin of newborn babies so that they can be monitored and tracked by FEMA officials. Activist Mark Koernke claims that he has documentation that these "chips" are actually bombs that can be detonated "anytime the government wants to produce a little terror among the population."

And then there is the matter of the strange designs on the back of one-dollar bills. Some militia members believe that the pyramid and the eye hovering above it is in reality a devilish mark of what they contend is the Jewish-controlled Federal Reserve. Others say the currency itself has bar codes on it so that government agents can drive by houses and, using scanners, determine how much money each family has.

"Whether they believe these ideas or not, I think a great many militia members are smart enough to realize that these kinds of conspiracy theories don't do much for their movement among the public," says analyst Terence Kirby. "Unlike some of their ideas, which a reasonable person *might* feel warrant a second or third look, these sound almost delusional."

As for the Patriots who circulate such notions, even some of their fellow militia members scoff at the wilder ideas. Even so, they rarely dismiss their fellow militia members as crazy. "No, they don't speak for me," says Adam Halloran of a Wisconsin militia.

> I don't believe in exploding biochips or that we're being scanned to see how much cash we've got on us. But hey—that doesn't mean it *couldn't* happen, or that the government wouldn't do it if they could get away with it. I've learned to listen to everybody these days. I mean, the media twists things around so much, I guess most of the time I'd listen to a patriot more than the six o'clock news.

4

Being in a Militia Today

EXPERTS AGREE THAT the number of people in today's militias has grown substantially in the past few years, although they also say that to categorize all militias as racist or anti-Semitic would be inaccurate. "There is no doubt that the militias themselves were founded by individuals who were both racist and anti-Semitic," says sociologist Lawrence Evans. "And because their membership pretty much reflected those views—and all the paranoia that went with them—few people took them seriously."

However, Evans cautions, in the past two years a lot has changed. "What we're seeing are militias overhauling their image, assuring people that they're not racists or bigots—just patriots who love their country." Devin Burghart, a researcher for the Coalition for Human Dignity, which tracks right-wing groups, agrees wholeheartedly. "Getting up and talking publicly about race separation are political methods that belong to the past. . . . But that doesn't change the fact that the organizing [of militias] . . . is being done by traditional racists."

Take a look, say those who keep track of militia activity, at the almost homogenous image of the Patriot groups and armed militias. Their membership includes a handful of Jews, even an African American here and there. But these exceptions are tolerated by most militia leaders, not recruited. And, says John Trochmann, founder of the Militia of Montana, their positions in the militias aren't permanent. "I'm following God's law. Blacks, Jews are welcome. But when America is the new Israel, they'll need to go back where they came from. It's just nature's law—kind should go unto kind."

"A white male thing"

While many militias have recently pointed out their minority members to show that they are not racist or anti-Semitic, they have not expressed the same interest in having women as members. Not surprising, says Mike Reynolds of Klanwatch, which monitors militia and Patriot activity. "There is no room for women in the militia leadership. This is a white male thing."

Linda Thompson can speak of this exclusion from personal experience. Like Mark Koernke from the Michigan Militia and John Trochmann of the Militia of Montana, Thompson is considered one of the "celebrities" of the militia movement. Like Koernke and Trochmann, Thompson is known throughout the nation for her antigovernment views.

A man and woman sell bumper stickers at a rally protesting federal government policy.

Until recently, she was a self-described "dumpy broad" from Indianapolis, working as a civil rights attorney there. Today, however, she refers to herself as the Acting General of the Unorganized Militia of the United States of America. What accounts for this transformation? Thompson says that it started with the Ruby Ridge incident. She was appalled by the way the government conducted itself—as she sees it, attacking without provocation. "Something inside me just snapped," she says, shaking her head.

Thompson resolved that if ever another such incident occurred, she would not hesitate to get involved—and six months later, the Branch Davidian compound was stormed in Waco. She directed, wrote, and produced a video about the incident called *Waco, the Big Lie* that became an instant favorite with the growing militia groups around the country.

"*Stay home* where you belong!"

However, militia leaders criticized her for posting an Internet bulletin urging an armed militia to come to Washington, D.C., and arrest Congress for treason. (Thompson believes Congress acted illegally years ago in passing the Fourteenth and Sixteenth Amendments to the Constitution, putting restraints on states' rights and establishing the income tax.) There was no support for her idea from the militias. One militia newsletter printed an openly hostile letter to Thompson urging her to "*Stay home* where you belong!"

Despite Thompson's treatment, militia leaders say women have a place in the militias and Patriot groups. As proof, they present an essay often quoted by militia groups, entitled "Women *Do* Have a Part in the Days Ahead." In the essay, women are assured that their role can be an important one. For instance, women are urged to store food for the dangerous times to come. They must prepare the children to be obedient. "Don't have time?" the essayist asks. "How much time do you spend watching soap operas . . . or buying new clothes? *Make* time!" Another acceptable role is assisting their husbands by offering

Theresa Kahl is the information officer and survival tactics instructor for the Michigan Militia.

support and encouragement. "Nothing will give a man more spunk than to know he's got a woman back there cheering him on," the essay promises. "Pray for him every day. Be submissive and understanding."

Under the "soft umbrella"

As right-wing leaders learned in the months after the Ruby Ridge and Waco incidents, there are many who do not share their racist views but who do share a growing hatred and distrust of the federal government. And it is this group that most worries experts. They do not think of themselves as violent, nor do they feel they are anything other than good, middle-class people. "I love my country," says one, "it's the government I hate."

This hatred is bringing so-called average Americans into the Patriot movement, and, more alarmingly, into the armed militias. "People are drawn in [to militias] under this soft umbrella of anger at the government and soon are taken into the more violent part of the movement if they continue to express interest," declares an agent of the hate-group-monitoring Center for Democratic Renewal.

A member of the Arkansas Militia says that he joined because of what he calls "the gun grabbing" of the federal government, evident in the passage of the Brady Bill and other legislation restricting gun purchases. "I like to hunt, I like guns—so the whole thing with the [gun regulations] made me mad," he says.

This photo oddly juxtaposes the violence advocated by a militia member's shirt with the innocent face of his young child.

However, he admits that once inside the militia, many of its criticisms of the federal government as a whole struck home.

> I'd never really thought about it like that, but the more I did, I figured it could be just like they say—the government may be getting ready to take us prisoner, and the first step might be our guns. I'm not giving my gun up to anyone! What right has the federal government got to decide that I have to register my own property?
>
> I mean, it never ends—register for taxes, get licenses for dogs, for cars, for you name it. No way—those people don't represent *me*. . . . So I joined. I no longer feel that the American government represents me. So we [in the militia] are representing ourselves—and Washington better pay attention, that's what I say.

Aside from gun legislation, however, there are many reasons why more and more Americans seem to be taking a hard look at the federal government, and are coming away distrustful.

The angry farmers

Some of the anti–federal government voices belong to farmers who have experienced monumental financial problems since the 1980s, when most countries of the world experienced a staggering recession. At that time the money underdeveloped countries had been using to buy U.S. grain was diverted to repay international loans. "A surplus of American produce resulted," explains one expert, "which in turn sent crop prices and land values plummeting. Farmland once valued at $2,100 an acre crashed to less than $700 an acre."

Moreover, inflation made necessary farm supplies and equipment more expensive, and farmers were forced deep into debt. Many pledged their property as collateral on new loans, and the situation only got worse. Worried about collecting on their loans, banks gave farmers thirty to sixty days to repay, or face foreclosure. Many small and midsize farms were forced into bankruptcy and the sale of land, machinery, and homes. During the 1980s many Midwest states saw the failure of ten to fifteen farms a day, and many farmers who managed to survive were living well below the poverty line.

The farmers were not only baffled, they were furious; they held the government responsible for the financial crises that had ruined them. After all, just ten years earlier, the U.S. Department of Agriculture had encouraged farmers to take out large loans. "According to federal officials, those who took the advice would reap a bountiful harvest by purchasing more land and planting [crops from] fence to fence," says author Richard Abanes. "Many farmers trusted Uncle Sam, and against their better judgment buried themselves in debt, believing that bumper crops would more than lift them into profits."

Fury over federal regulations

The pool of unemployed Americans has also proved to be a significant source of recent recruits. Many jobs have been lost to cuts in government spending on, for example, defense, and as new federal regulations—especially those having to do with environmental issues—have gone into effect.

In Moab, Utah, for example, the key industry was uranium mining. (Uranium is used to produce nuclear power). When the Three Mile Island disaster occurred in 1979, the government reconsidered the role of nuclear power in America. The decision was to eliminate more than two thousand mining jobs in Moab, and "did ugly things to the temperament of this town," says a militia man from that area.

Environmentalists and environmental agencies are often cited as yet another threat to patriotic Americans. Events such as the closing of three large lumber mills in northern California in 1994—resulting from concern about spotted owl habitat—and mine closures elsewhere because of environmentalists' concerns about runoff hurting fish populations have brought more members into the militia fold.

"They're more worried about some little bug dying that they haven't even come up with a name for, than our jobs," said one California militia member with disgust. One

Militia members attend a "Preparedness Expo" in Dallas. Today, many people join a militia for no other reason than to give vent to their dissatisfaction with government actions and policies.

militant group from California published a list of its number-one enemies, and included, among others, "militant vegetarians . . . tree worshippers, animal rights goofballs . . . and human haters."

To all these disgruntled and angry people, the militias and Patriot groups offer the heady prospect of fighting back. Shrugs one militia leader from West Virginia, "We've never had to 'recruit' anyone at all. There are so many angry guys out there, guys who've been ridden over by 'The Beast' [federal government] and all its agencies. They just find us, word of mouth or whatever. And I'll say this—we get more and more members every month!"

Practice for the last battle

There are various ways in which those who join militias can stay in touch with one another and feel a part of what is going on. The most important contact is through meetings, held regularly from one to four times each month. Meetings are opportunities for talking and practicing war games. After all, says John Trochmann, "The security of a free state is not found in the citizens having guns in the closet—it's found in the citizenry being trained, prepared, organized, equipped, and led properly."

Most militias are secretive about their meetings, letting members know of upcoming events by mail or cryptic codes in telephone conversations. However, some groups openly advertise their activities in local newspapers and welcome newcomers. Before the members practice the various guerrilla and sniper techniques they've discussed in meetings, there is usually a discussion of rumors about any strange goings-on in the area, or perhaps detailed explanations of the newest in technical equipment or weaponry. Those connected with the Militia of Montana, for example, are reminded to "keep close and study" certain technical handbooks, such as *The Art of War, Guerrilla Warfare, and Special Forces Ops* or *Unconventional Warfare Devices and Techniques.*

Members are instructed repeatedly to have within arm's reach the "basics": an AR-15 semiautomatic rifle, a combat knife, and a minimum of six hundred rounds of .223 ammunition. The basics do not include the caches of weapons hidden in forests and mountains near some militia headquarters around the United States. Here are stockpiled not only guns, but more sophisticated weapons such as grenades, missiles, and rocket launchers. FBI agents suspect a few militias—including those in Montana—have the capability to withstand even chemical and biological warfare. As one militia leader brags, "We now have enough to hold off an entire battalion."

For instant communication, militia members in some of the most remote areas of Montana and Idaho carry two-way radios. One leader explained, "Many, many people—I won't say how many, but a lot—have these radios, and we stay tuned to a certain frequency, a certain channel, and our radios are always on."

Catalogs and conventions

Besides meetings, there are other ways militia members can keep in touch with one another, or can at least be kept abreast of recent developments. Mailings are an important function of the leaders of militias. In addition to communicating news of interest to enemies of the New World Order, including up-to-date information on conspiracy theories, the mailings spread the militia movement across the country.

The largest distributor of such mailings is the Militia of Montana, widely known as MOM. David Trochmann, the brother of MOM leader John Trochmann, is in charge of the militia's mailings. Much of what he sends out are start-up kits for others wishing to build militias. According to David Trochmann, he often fills orders for two hundred start-up kits each week, including pamphlets, videotapes, and books, all shipped in large cardboard boxes. "I've carried as many as 16 boxes in one day," he says, "all filled with this stuff. Our shipping costs generally run to $200 bucks per day, and we've had it go as high as $1,200 bucks."

Since 1995 some of the larger militias have sponsored or participated in conventions around the United States. "We use it to recruit, to educate people who aren't sure what

A self-published handbook for the militia man is sold at a convention. Such conventions are a way for militias to get the word out to potential members.

we're about," says Indiana militia member Bob Gross. "We have speakers, sell pamphlets, talk to folks. It's a lot of work, but really gratifying, you know?"

Sometimes celebrities of the movement such as Mark Koernke and John Trochmann attend: At a recent convention in Big Falls, Montana, Koernke instructed a standing-room-only crowd on the use of nylon rope to hang legislators. Many shows offer visitors instructional classes: In doing research for his book *Warrior Dreams*, sociologist James Gibson enrolled in a class on combat pistol training. He was surprised, he said, that he and the other men in the session were taught even "how the warrior should go to the bathroom." Forget urinals, ordered the instructor, for they leave you vulnerable to attack from behind. The correct technique, Gibson learned, was "to sit on a toilet with a pistol between your legs, ready to fire on anybody who tries to invade your stall."

Enthusiasts can spend a great deal of money at such conventions: Various vendors offer for sale everything from related books, videos, and T-shirts, to Uzis and

Michigan Militia leader Mark Koernke (second from left) attends a militia rally. People who are contemplating joining a militia are often enticed to such rallies by the chance to see people like Koernke.

chemical warfare suits. One of the big sellers at T-shirt booths during the summer of 1996 displayed a skull and dagger and the words: "Kill 'Em All, Let God Sort 'Em Out." And a popular videotape called *The Pestilence* told how the New World Order was planning on using the AIDS virus to exterminate 2 billion people by the year 2000.

For seventy-five dollars one can buy a training manual that explains not only the biblical justifications for a guerrilla war in the United States, but also detailed instructions on how such a war can be won. The manual describes how to raid armories to steal ammunition and weapons, mount sabotage attacks on factories and communications systems to cripple the American economy, and conduct domestic terrorism including bombings and arson.

The eleven- and eighteen-year-old daughters of Steve Brown, chair of the Texas State Militia, sell information at a regional militia rally in San Antonio.

"Just us flexing our muscles a little"

However, it is becoming obvious to the public—especially in those areas in which militias are active—that militia members are doing more than attending meetings, going to conventions, and watching videos about the New World Order. In recent months there have been numerous instances of people who have been threatened or attacked by militia members. "We are not dealing with a bunch of good old boys playing war games down by the creek," warns one county sheriff in Washington. "They're really serious about what they're doing, and anybody who underestimates them is not paying attention."

Many of these incidents have involved federal employees who have attempted to enforce laws unpopular with local militias. Agents of the U.S. Forest Service and the Bureau of Land Management have been the most frequent targets, although local police, legislators, and judges have also been threatened, harassed, and even shot, their offices or homes destroyed by explosions or fire.

In Nevada, Forest Service workers trying to enforce new environmental laws prohibiting ranchers from grazing cattle on federal land have been fired upon and intimidated by mobs of angry people identifying themselves only as individuals "who have been forced to uphold the Constitution against traitors in the government." At a public meeting in Ely, Nevada, a local rancher threatened to shoot an official from the Bureau of Land Management. One witness said, "He stood up and told the agent that if he had only two bullets left, he would save one of them for him."

A judge from Hamilton, Montana, learned that a militia group had put out a contract on her life after she refused to allow a member of the group to pursue a claim that the government had no jurisdiction over him. She was threatened by dozens of letters and phone calls, followed when she was driving to and from work, and warned that she would be kidnapped and brought before a militia court, where she would be tried and executed for her treasonous acts. Federal law enforcement agencies concluded that the threats were not idle and urged the judge to take her

children and leave the country until they could apprehend those who were responsible for the death threats.

"Those threats are nothing," said one anonymous letter. "This is just the beginning, just the salad before the main meal. This is just us flexing our muscles a little. What's to come will be more terrible than anything this country can imagine."

"Get me with your first shot"

Such incidents have had sad consequences for many people connected with government agencies. In parts of the country where militias are an active presence, such workers are treated with contempt by area residents. Forest Service agents say that their children are taunted by classmates, that no one will share pews with them in church, and that they frequently are the victims of vandalism to their homes and cars. In various towns in Nevada, there are signs in cafés and diners stating "No Federal Employee Will Be Served." In numerous cases, Patriots and militia members have vowed to shoot not only the workers, but their young children as well.

"It's a lonely way to live," said the wife of a Forest Service worker. "We're basically the pariahs out here. I don't like answering the phone, because the voices scare me. And I worry about [my husband] all the time, him being out there in a car with a government insignia right on the door. I wish they'd scrape those insignias off—they're making the officers targets, I think, just sitting ducks."

County sheriffs and other law enforcement officers feel the same way. One county marshal admitted that he now thinks two or three times about stopping certain vehicles for routine traffic violations. "If I know the guy is part of [a militia], I know he's probably got a couple of guns and 500 rounds of ammunition. I think, do I want to risk my life pulling him over, or even serving a warrant on a guy like that? Is it worth it, having to shoot him, or having one of my deputies shot over something like that?"

Officials know the feeling in many remote towns is that the government is the enemy. They know, too, that many militia members have sworn that they will never allow themselves to be captured alive. "Don't wound me, kill me," one man threatened a county sheriff in Idaho. "Get me with your first shot—that's the only way you can stop me."

5

The Threat Among Us

THE THREATS AND vandalism pale, however, before the April 19, 1995, bombing of the Alfred P. Murrah Federal Building in Oklahoma City. The blast killed 169 people, including 19 children in the day-care center on the building's second floor. More than 600 people were injured. It was the worst terrorist attack in U.S. history.

Because of the way the bombing was accomplished—using a truck filled with explosives—investigators first suspected Arab terrorists, since this method is a signature of some Middle East terrorist groups. The public, too, was quick to jump to the same conclusions, and for a short time, there was a flurry of hate directed at Arab Americans on the streets and on the airwaves.

What kind of American?

Within hours of the blast, however, federal investigators found what one expert called "an indelible trail of evidence" leading to an American, a twenty-seven-year-old former infantryman named Timothy McVeigh. McVeigh, it was soon learned, rented the truck used in the bombing. He was found to have traces of chemicals on his clothes and in his car that were linked to the explosives used in the bombing. In addition, he was reported to have told his friend Terry Nichols—also under investigation for the crime—that "something big" was going to happen soon. McVeigh also is said to have promised his sister that he was going to do "something" on April 19.

News reports showed the mangled bodies of men, women, and children being removed from the rubble of the federal building, and throughout the United States, people grieved. The grief was mixed with confusion and anger as Americans learned that the bombing appeared to be the act of at least one domestic terrorist. What kind of American would do such a thing, would kill innocent people?

Streets are clogged with traffic after the bombing of the Oklahoma City federal building.

Militia ties

In the weeks following the tragedy in Oklahoma City, investigators gathered more information about their chief suspect. McVeigh, they say, fits the profile of a right-wing extremist. He is an avowed racist and anti-Semite. He has links to Aryan Nations, Christian Identity, the Arizona Patriots, and the Michigan Militia, although a Michigan Militia spokesman quickly disavowed any ties to McVeigh and Nichols, whom he said "were silenced. . . . In fact, they were told to leave."

Oklahoma City bombing suspect Timothy McVeigh is led from the courthouse by FBI agents.

Federal authorities describe McVeigh as an avid gun collector and a regular participant at right-wing conventions. One acquaintance said that McVeigh had numerous copies of neo-Nazi William Pierce's *The Turner Diaries*, which he sold at gun shows. He was apparently obsessed by the government's actions at Ruby Ridge and Waco. FBI photographs show McVeigh among Davidian supporters who showed up at Waco. He was an avid listener to the talk-radio show of Mark Koernke, a man whom some have described as "close to McVeigh." McVeigh has not confessed; in fact, he has adamantly refused to talk to investigators. When asked a question, he repeats only his name, rank, and date of birth, in the manner prescribed by the manual of the Michigan Militia for "prisoners of war."

It is important to note that federal investigators have found no evidence that directly links the bombing with any particular group. Even so, the philosophies and hate-filled politics of McVeigh have forced Americans to take a long, hard look at the many thousands of others with the same views.

Not a shock to everyone

While most Americans reacted to the Oklahoma City bombing with shock and outrage, some were not surprised at all. Some people connected with watchdog agencies such as the Southern Poverty Law Center and the American Jewish Committee even anticipated such an attack. Kenneth S. Stern, the AJC's expert on hate groups, says that he had documented his fears just days before the bombing. "I had written that people connected with militias were poised to attack government officials," he writes in *A Force upon the Plain*, "possibly on April 19, 1995, the second anniversary of the fiery end of the Branch Davidian compound in Waco."

Morris Dees of the Southern Poverty Law Center wrote to Janet Reno, U.S. attorney general, in October 1994, that the militia movement posed a serious threat to American safety. Says Dees, "I wrote to alert her to the danger posed by the growing number of radical militia groups." Dees had learned that some of the nation's most notorious racists and anti-Semites were infiltrating the leadership of the militias. "I told the attorney general that this 'mixture of armed groups and those who hate was a recipe for disaster.'"

However, such warnings were not heeded. Neither federal law enforcement agencies nor Congress was aware of the huge stockpiles of weapons and ammunition held by those in the militia movement. They *were* aware of the antigovernment rhetoric that Patriot and militia groups were generating. However, they were not aware of either the extent of the militias' violent intentions or the sophistication of their weaponry.

Even the ATF, the federal agency most hated by the militias, dismissed them as basically harmless, more bark than bite. According to one ATF official, "You can have horrible beliefs in this country and make horrible statements and not be a matter for federal investigation."

Some in the FBI and other federal agencies blamed the strict laws protecting militias' freedom of speech and assembly. They say that such protections make it difficult for them to effectively infiltrate and monitor such groups, or even to move against suspects until it is too late to prevent a crime. Others admit that the agencies were purposely reluctant to move, intending to avoid public criticism and lawsuits like those that resulted from what was called the agency's overzealousness in the past, including the handling of Ruby Ridge and Waco.

Varied reactions from militias

How did militia and Patriot leaders react when the spotlight focused on them? Many on the "softer edges" of militias immediately distanced themselves from the groups, unwilling to be associated with the horrifying news videos of bleeding and mangled children being carried from the rubble of the federal building. Some militia leaders even condemned the action. Norm Olson, then leader of the Michigan Militia, stated, "There is no justification for bru-

Former Michigan Militia leader Norm Olson condemned the Oklahoma City bombing. Many militia leaders throughout the country agreed with Olson.

tality meeting brutality." The leader of a Utah militia disbanded his group, saying that the bombing "sickened and disgusted us—it is far from what anybody in [our group] would ever condone."

However, some experts say that much of the outrage expressed by militias was insincere. One man who had been actively involved with several militias around the country reported that behind closed doors "many members speak of the Oklahoma City bombing with pride, and have made McVeigh their new martyr." Another militia member who attended a Patriot convention in Branson, Missouri, just two days after the bombing, agreed. As he saw it, many militia members felt that the bombing was an understandable reaction to the 1993 deaths of the children in the Branch Davidian compound. "I mingled with a lot of people [at the convention]," he said, "and there was not a shred of sympathy for what happened in Oklahoma."

Some Patriots, on the other hand, were far from secretive about their approval of the bombing. "The bombing was a fine thing," remarked Dennis Mahon of the White Aryan Resistance. "I hate the federal government. . . . I'm surprised that this hasn't happened all over the country." Patriot leader Bo Gritz expressed his admiration for the technical skill of the bomber, saying, "It was a Rembrandt— a masterpiece of science and art put together."

New conspiracies

However, the most common feeling on the part of militia members was that the bombing was in fact orchestrated by the federal government itself. Randy Trochmann of the Militia of Montana (the twenty-seven-year-old nephew of MOM leader John Trochmann) believes its purpose was to divert attention from the scandals associated with the president and first lady.

"Hard to say what happened," Trochmann said days after the bombing, "but I will tell you this: If it hadn't been for the bombing, the headlines would have read 'Bill and Hillary Clinton Subpoenaed to Testify on Whitewater.' Instead, *that* news got buried."

Others concur in the sentiment expressed by Trochmann, although they offer different reasons. "All the new gun grab laws were stalling in Congress, and they were losing support fast," says one Illinois militia member. "This was a way to really get people scared about guns, so that legislation would pass." A spokesman for a California militia feels the blame rests entirely on the New World Order. "This was orchestrated by the shadow government [FEMA, the UN, etc.]," he says, "to whip the public into such a frenzy that Americans will BEG to surrender their privacy for some government-provided protection from terrorism."

Linda Thompson says there is no question that the federal government bombed its own citizens. And, she maintains, the fact that nineteen children died in the explosion would not have bothered the government at all. "After all," she says confidently, "who's got a track record of killing innocent children?"

Mark Koernke has been the most outspoken militia supporter since the bombing. As a firm believer that the New World Order is coming soon, Koernke is convinced that its agents carried out the bombing. He contends that television footage supports his claim. "As a matter of fact," he stated publicly after the bombing, "[my wife] Nancy and the kids, watching the initial footage of this, saw what appeared to be United Nations observers' badges." Koernke also urged others to videotape the site and document which agencies they saw coming in and out of the site.

"We never know who is listening"

Reckless and sometimes vicious talk on certain radio shows has prompted worry in Washington, D.C., and elsewhere. These shows, some believe, may incite domestic terrorism among those who hate and mistrust government.

For instance, conservative talk-show host G. Gordon Liddy gave his listeners some alarming advice less than a month after the Oklahoma bombing. He warned the public about the increasing possibility of federal agents invading private homes in the coming months. When shooting at them, Liddy warned, be thrifty with your ammunition. "You've got a big target on there . . . [which]

"What do you mean, the government's out to get you? It's already *got* you."

says 'ATF.' Don't shoot at them, because they got a vest on underneath that. Head shots, head shots! . . . Kill the sons of bitches!"

Another radio program, *Love of Truth*, is a Christian Identity show hosted by a militia leader named Mark Reynolds. Said Reynolds during one of his broadcasts, "Laws to execute [homosexuals] would surely put a quick end to people dying from AIDS they got in a restaurant or the dentist's chair! So-called tolerance," he went on, "is anti-Christian." In another program he warned that if the federal government continued to be as heavy-handed as it is currently, "people like [Attorney General Janet] Reno will end up hanging from telephone poles or trees."

"Who do we shoot?"

And radio host Chuck Baker, broadcasting from Colorado Springs, wondered aloud, "The problem we have right now is who do we shoot? . . . Other members of Congress are borderline traitors. They're the kingpins right now, beside the Slick One [President Clinton]. . . . You've got to get your ammo."

After the tragedy in Oklahoma City, a few radio station general managers became nervous about the content of certain shows on their stations and pulled them off the air, prompting in many cases such outraged reaction from loyal listeners that the decision was quickly reversed. Bo Gritz's show, for example, was canceled the week after the bombing, but the station was barraged with so many calls, he was back on the air in forty-eight hours.

Many experts warn that such inflammatory talk on the public airwaves presents a very real danger of leading certain individuals to violence. After the Oklahoma bombing, Clinton denounced some for making a bad situation worse by keeping people "as paranoid as possible, and the rest of us all torn up and upset with each other." He continued, "We should be careful about the kind of language we use and the kind of incendiary talk we engage in. We never know who is listening or what impact it might have. So we need to show some restraint and discipline because of all

the people in this country that might be on the edge and might be capable of doing something horrible like this."

Expanding

Besides the glut of antigovernment hate talk in the months since the Oklahoma bombing, many are worried about the expansion of the militias and Patriot groups. "It's hard to believe, with all that attention that the media has paid them—almost all of it negative—they are growing, not shrinking," said a county sheriff from Idaho.

But militias are not worried by what some dismiss as bad press. A spokesman for the Militia of Montana shrugs happily, "After *48 Hours* did that piece on us, we got 400 calls from people wanting to join," he says. "Every day there are more reasons to join us." And Mark Koernke denies that the bombing has hurt the Michigan Militia. "Since Oklahoma our activity has ratcheted up threefold," he says. "My speaking schedule is busier than ever."

Another important reason for their growth is increasingly coordinated information gathering and distribution. Since Oklahoma, more than thirty militias, together with

New members are sworn into a militia. The increasing membership of militias, especially in the wake of the Oklahoma City bombing, worries officials who believe they pose a threat to the United States.

the neo-Nazi group Aryan Nations, have merged their resources by computer. Computer bulletin boards and Internet postings have carried recipes for bombs. In West Milford, New Jersey, two twelve-year-olds recently made napalm, a jelling agent for incendiary devices, from a recipe they took from computer postings. Three weeks before the Oklahoma bombing, one posting described in complete detail how to make an ammonium nitrate bomb, the type used to blow up the federal building. Media experts estimate that there are three hundred militia and Patriot bulletin boards on the Internet, and that because such messages and directions can be posted anonymously, there is almost no risk involved for purveyors.

No easy way

Many experts today agree that militias pose a very real threat to the safety of Americans. Something must be done, they say, to regulate militia activity and thus minimize domestic terrorism.

Some advocate state laws making militia activity of any size illegal. Twenty-four states had such laws as of 1996. The laws, however, are meaningless unless they are vigorously enforced. With proper enforcement, much can be accomplished. For instance, Klan paramilitary camps were closed down in Texas when citizen organizations such as the Southern Poverty Law Center filed suits. The same thing happened in North Carolina, when the White Patriot Party tried to operate military organizations.

But many state legislators and state prosecutors are uneasy about passing and enforcing such laws. They feel nervous confronting groups of armed citizens who have threatened violence, and who have acted on such threats. It takes a great deal of courage to pass and enforce legislation, says Morris Dees, and it will have its cost. "But the cost of not moving firmly will be higher," he warns.

Yet others feel that such confrontation will have a far more negative effect. It is precisely heavy-handed behavior by law enforcement, they say, that turned Ruby Ridge and Waco into such volatile incidents. Given the kinds of fears militia members have of government, cracking down on them by legislation and confrontation might only escalate tensions to far more dangerous levels.

Willing to die

No matter how the challenge presented by militias in America is met, experts are unanimous in their beliefs that the United States cannot afford to approach militias lightly. "These are people who believe strongly in what they are doing," says one psychologist who has studied militia activity.

> The vast majority are people who, for whatever reason, feel passionately that their country is going in a direction that is wrong, and that the system no longer will work for them. They feel just as passionately that they should take matters into their own hands. . . . And the thing that should be utmost in our minds is that many of them are more than ready, more than willing to die for their passion.

Carolyn Trochmann, the wife of Militia of Montana leader John Trochmann, would wholeheartedly agree. She says she knows her family has chosen a very different path than other Americans. "These people are ignorant," she says matter-of-factly of the people in her Montana town. And she is totally at peace, even with her view of what's to come. "I know my husband will be killed," she says, "and I have made my peace with that fact. It's his destiny. I'm proud of my family."

Organizations
to Contact

American Civil Liberties Union (ACLU)
122 Maryland Ave. NE
Washington, DC 20002
(202) 544-1681

The ACLU is a national organization that works to defend the civil rights of Americans as guaranteed in the U.S. Constitution. The organization is critical of many antiterrorist bills, believing that such legislation would limit the rights and freedoms of citizens.

Anti-Defamation League of B'nai B'rith
100 Connecticut Ave. NW, Suite 1020
Washington, DC 20036
(202) 857-6660

This Jewish organization seeks to combat anti-Semitism and bigotry in its many forms in the United States and around the world. It has served as a watchdog agency, monitoring neo-Nazi and white supremacist groups.

Bureau of Alcohol, Tobacco, and Firearms (ATF)
650 Massachusetts Ave. NW, Suite 8100
Washington, DC 20226
(202) 927-7777

Part of the Treasury Department, the ATF enforces and administers laws relating to alcohol, tobacco, firearms, explosives, and destructive devices such as bombs. It also investigates criminal activities relating to such materials.

Federal Bureau of Investigation (FBI)

Counterterrorism Branch
10th St. and Pennsylvania Ave. NW, Suite 5222
Washington, DC 20535
(202) 329-3000

The FBI is the federal law enforcement agency with primary jurisdiction over counterterrorism activities of the U.S. government. It also investigates activities of known terrorists operating in the United States.

Klanwatch Project

P.O. Box 548
Montgomery, AL 36104-0548
(334) 265-8335

Funded through the Southern Poverty Law Center, this organization gathers information on the activities of militias and other right-wing extremist organizations operating in the United States. It publishes a bimonthly newsletter, "Klanwatch Intelligence Report."

Louisiana Patriots

17588 Simpson Rd.
Prairieville, LA 70769

This group is a part of the extreme right in the United States, and believes in the racist and anti-Semitic doctrines of Christian Identity. The Louisiana Patriots are advocates of the notion of the coming of the New World Order. They publish a bimonthly newsletter.

Militia of Montana (MOM)

P.O. Box 1486
Noxon, MT 59853

MOM is the largest and most well organized of the U.S. militias. It publishes catalogs and newsletters and distributes information for those interested in starting their own regional militias.

Suggestions for Further Reading

Michael Barone, "A Brief History of Zealotry in America," *U.S. News & World Report*, May 8, 1995.

Marc Cooper, "Montana's Mother of All Militias," *Nation*, May 22, 1995.

James Corcoran, *Bitter Harvest: Gordon Kahl and the Posse Comitatus—Murder in the Heartland*. New York: Penguin Books, 1990.

"The Enemy Within," *Maclean's*, May 8, 1995.

Kevin Flynn and Gary Gerhardt, *The Silent Brotherhood*. New York: Penguin Books, 1989.

Denis Johnson, "The Militia in Me," *Esquire*, July 1995.

Michael Kelly, "The Road to Paranoia," *New Yorker*, June 19, 1995.

Gary E. McCuen, ed., *The Militia Movement and Hate Groups in America*. Hudson, WI: Gary McCuen Publications, 1996.

Carl Mollins, "At Home with a Racist Guru," *Maclean's*, May 8, 1995.

"Neo-Nazi's Terrorist Novel: Likely Blueprint for Oklahoma Bombers," *Klanwatch*, June 1995.

Pat Robertson, *The New World Order*. Dallas: Word Publishing, 1991.

Jill Smolowe, "Enemies of the State," *Time*, May 8, 1995.

Rogers Worthington, "Private Militias March to the Beat of Deep Distrust," *Chicago Tribune*, September 25, 1994.

Works Consulted

Richard Abanes, *American Militias: Rebellion, Racism & Religion*. Downer's Grove, IL: Intervarsity Press, 1996.

Morris Dees, *Gathering Storm: America's Militia Threat*. New York: HarperCollins, 1996.

"An Epidemic of Fear and Loathing," *U.S. News & World Report*, May 8, 1995.

James William Gibson, *Warrior Dreams: Paramilitary Culture in Post-Vietnam America*. New York: Hill and Wang, 1994.

Thomas Halpern and Brian Levin, *The Limits of Dissent: The Constitutional Status of Armed Civilian Militias*. Amherst, MA: Aletheia Press, 1996.

Philip Jenkins, "Home Grown Terror," *American Heritage*, September 1995.

Lyman Tower Sergeant, ed., *Extremism in America*. New York: New York University Press, 1995.

Kenneth S. Stern, *A Force upon the Plain*. New York: Simon and Schuster, 1996.

Jess Walter, *Every Knee Shall Bow: The Truth & Tragedy of Ruby Ridge and the Randy Weaver Family*. New York: Regan Books, 1995.

Index

About the Author

Gail B. Stewart received her undergraduate degree from Gustavus Adolphus College in St. Peter, Minnesota. She did her graduate work in English, linguistics, and curriculum study at the College of St. Thomas and the University of Minnesota. She taught English and reading for more than ten years.

She has written over ninety books for young people, including a series for Lucent Books called The Other America. She has written many books on historical topics such as World War I and the Warsaw Ghetto.

Stewart and her husband live in Minneapolis with their three sons, Ted, Elliot, and Flynn, two dogs, and a cat. When she is not writing she enjoys reading, walking, and watching her sons play soccer.

Picture Credits